Published by Ladybird Books Ltd 2011
A Penguin Company
Penguin Books Ltd, 80 Strand, London, WC2R 0RL, UK
Penguin Books Australia Ltd, Camberwell, Victoria, Australia
Penguin Books (NZ), 67 Apollo Drive, Rosedale, Auckland 0632, New Zealand
(a division of Pearson New Zealand Ltd)

www.ladybird.com

ISBN: 978-1-40930-934-5
001 - 10 9 8 7 6 5 4 3 2 1
Printed in Poland

THE OFFICIAL LEGO® ANNUAL 2012

CONTENTS

Countdown!

5 . . . 4 . . . 3 . . . 2 . . . 1 . . . LIFT OFF! Circle the two numbers in each row that can be added to make the rocket launch countdown number on the left.

Spot the parts:
4x
3x
Can you also spot six people with blue hats?
L336 - 8
Octan

Space Trail

Follow the trails in space to find out which spaceship has taken off from the moon and which one from Earth.

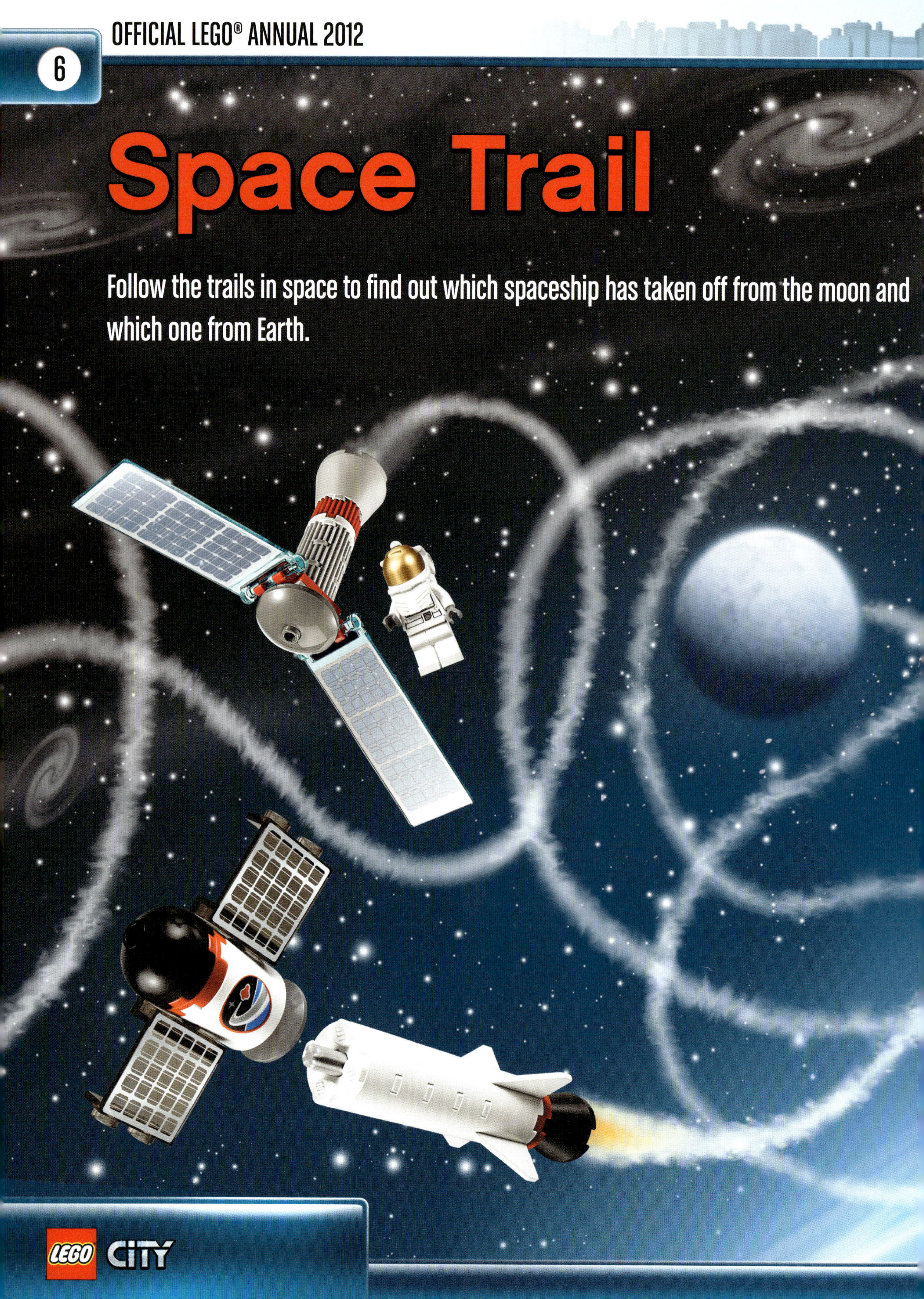

JM 3367

Wanted!

Help the LEGO® CITY police catch a crook. Use the police notes to put together the correct pieces of the crook's head. Then, put him in jail by drawing the prison bars without taking your pen off the page!

- he was seen wearing a grey hat
- he's got a gold tooth
- his eyebrows are not brown
- he's got a moustache and sideburns

POLICE
POLICE
POLICE
POLICE
HA 7285
WANTED!
START
POLICE

The Great Chase

Two crooks have robbed the bank and two LEGO CITY police officers are in hot pursuit. Can you help the policemen catch the crooks before they escape from the city?

Hop on the bike and ride it to the next square!

You're hungry! Miss a turn while you grab a bite to eat.

A shortcut! Climb up or down the ladder to the next square.

A game for 2 players. You will need two coins to use as game pieces and a dice. Take turns to roll the dice and move your game piece across the board, in the direction of the arrows. If you land on a picture square, read the key at the top and follow the instructions. The first player to reach the finish catches the crooks and wins the game!

Red light! Go back one space and miss a turn.

An urgent phone call from your mum! Go back to the start.

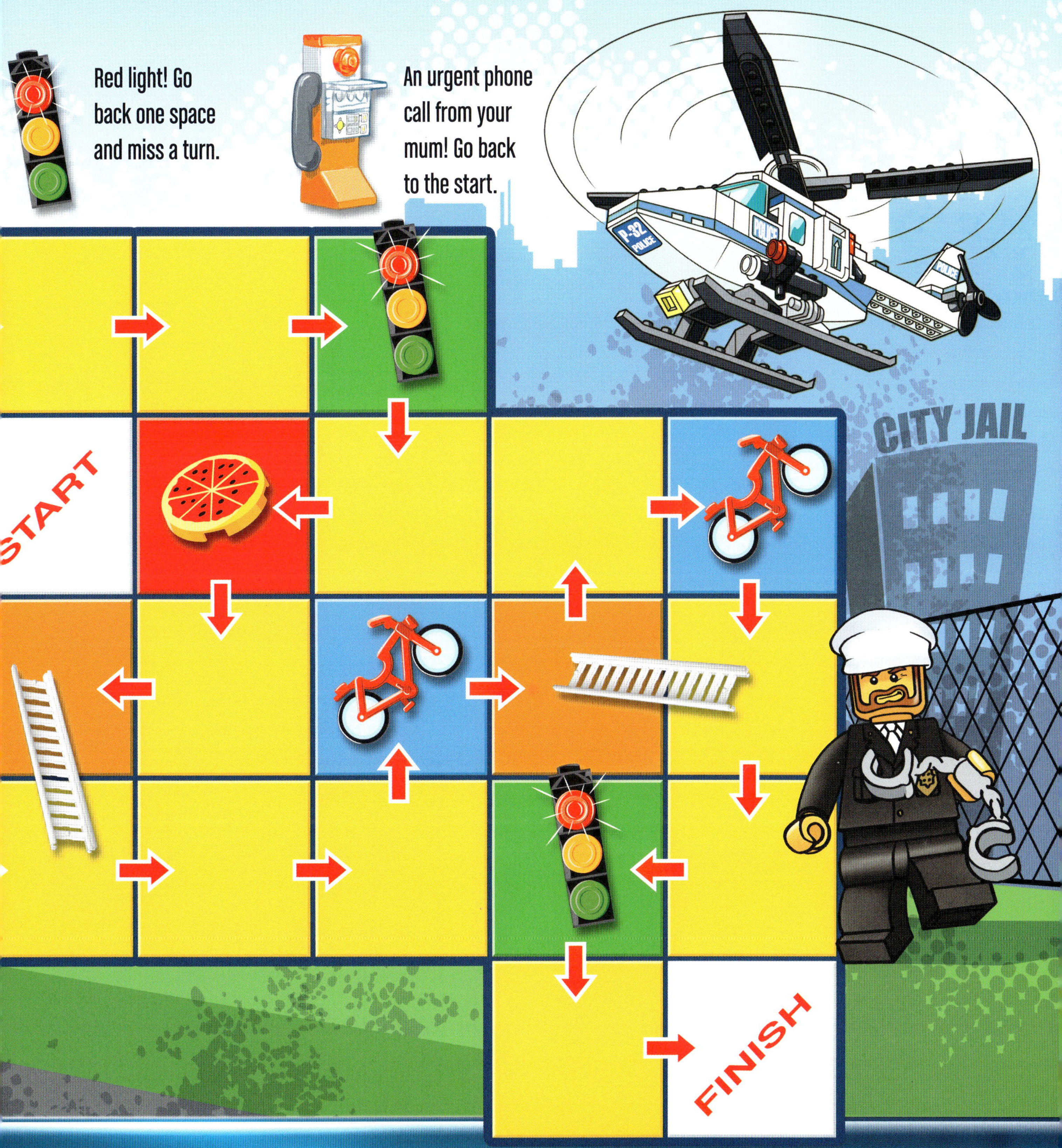

NICE CATCH
I KNOW HOW TO GET AWAY FROM THE POLICE!

I'LL GRAB HOLD OF THIS . . .

JUMP ON HERE . . .
4645

THEN SURF AWAY!

HEY!

WHAT
A BEAUTIFUL DAY . . .

. . . FOR FISHING!

HUH?

WHOOSH!

THUD

HAVE YOU EVER THOUGHT OF WORKING FOR THE POLICE?

The Beach

Play this territory game with a friend to claim the beach! Take turns drawing a line between two dots. Every time you form a square, write your initials in it. Try to collect as many squares as you can containing a shell. The winner is the player who collects the most shells!

At The Harbour

LEGO CITY harbour is always busy. Can you circle the two small pictures below that do not belong in the big picture?

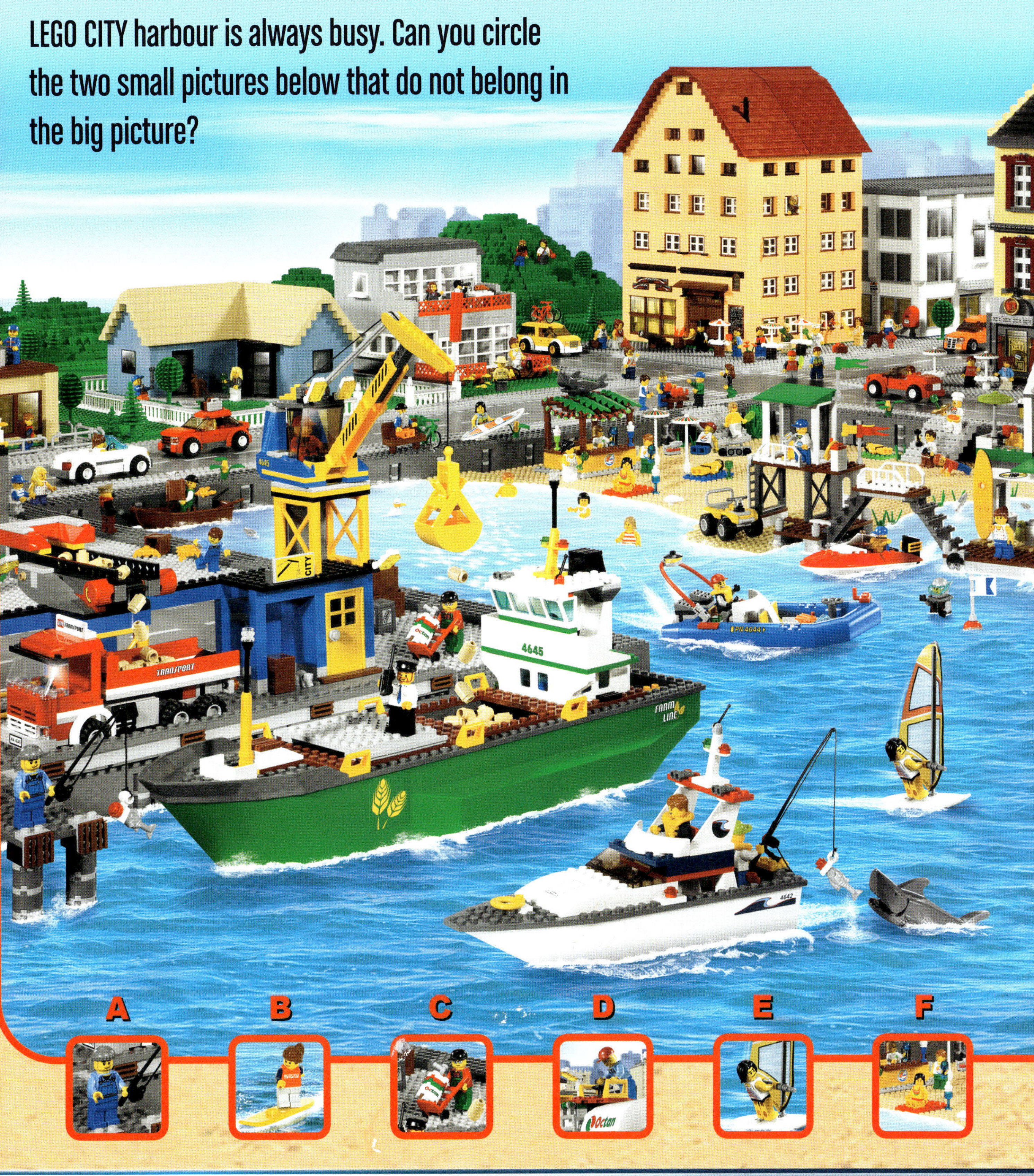

LEGO® CITY Stars

What's your favourite food?

- Doughnuts → You would paint your car . . .
- Hot dogs → What gives you the biggest thrills?
- Hot wings →

You would paint your car . . .

- Blue → At a costume ball you'd be dressed as . . .
- Red → What gives you the biggest thrills?

What gives you the biggest thrills?

- A treasure hunt → At a costume ball you'd be dressed as . . .
- A climbing wall → You most enjoy . . .
- A rollercoaster ride →

Walk your own path → What gives you the biggest thrills?

At a costume ball you'd be dressed as . . .

- A sheriff from the Wild West → When you drive your car, you would . . .
- A medieval knight → You most enjoy . . .

When you drive your car, you would . . .

- Burn the tyres → You most enjoy . . .
- Respect the law → You would love to get . . .

You most enjoy . . .

- Playing with friends → What's more exciting?

Chasing crooks → When you drive your car, you would . . .

You would love to get . . .

- A medal for courage → What's more exciting?
- A detective badge → POLICEMAN

What's more exciting?

- Chasing crooks → When you drive your car, you would . . .
- Fighting fires → FIRE FIGHTER

POLICEMAN

LEGO CITY police need someone like you! You could be great at solving puzzles.

FIRE FIGHTER

Great! You can't wait to join the action, and "courage" is your middle name.

Who could you be in LEGO CITY? Take this test and find out!

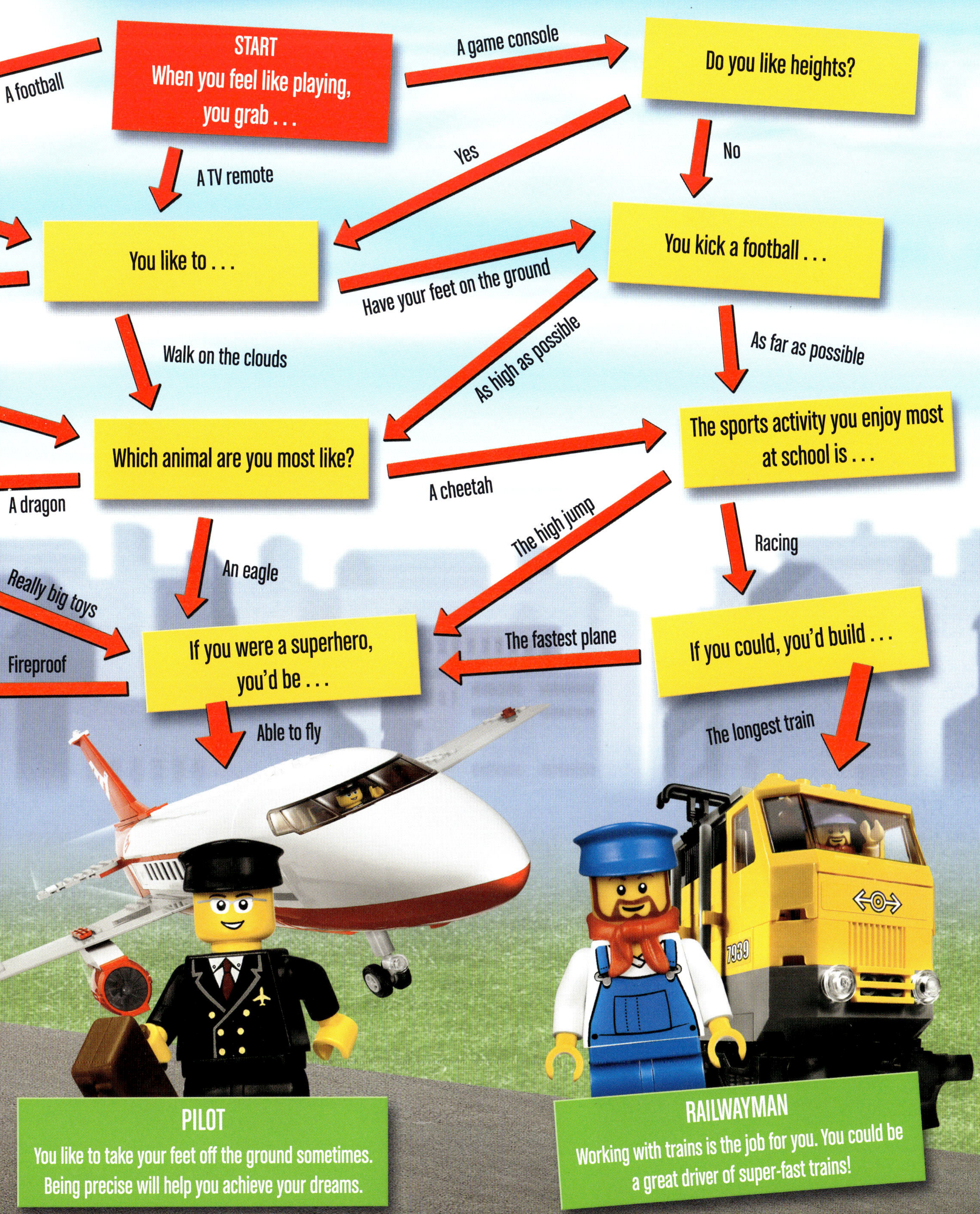

FIRE IN SPACE
SPACE SHUTTLE CALLING EARTH! THE LAUNCH WAS SUCCESSFUL – WE'RE IN ORBIT!

ALL SYSTEMS LOOKING GOOD – LET'S TAKE A QUICK BREAK.

I'D LIKE TO PROPOSE A TOAST WITH SOME HOT CHOCOLATE!

ALERT! ALERT! METEOR STORM!

OH, GOSH!

SPLASH!!!

LOOK WHAT YOU'VE DONE!
IT WAS AN ACCIDENT!

OUT OF THE WAY!

YOU KNOW THAT ONLY ASTRONAUTS WITH A LICENCE MAY USE THE SIMULATOR! NOW GO BACK TO YOUR CLASSROOM.
SIMULATOR

Weird Science

This scientist only needs two of the test tubes below for his crazy experiment. Circle the two tubes that will fill up one tube and turn green when mixed together.

Hidden Shapes

Four objects that belong to four characters at the bottom of the page have been cleverly hidden in this artist's painting. Colour in all the areas with dots to see the objects and circle the character whose object is missing.

Sports Rap!

Can you guess what sport these characters play? Match the rapper's rhymes with the correct sportsperson.

Yo, dudes!
Do you know who I'm rapping about?

His helmet is tough and he slides on the ice, when he hits the puck, he doesn't have to try twice.
3

She's dancing on ice, her skirt's in a spin. The best pirouette will decide if she wins.
4

Two very big guys with their hair in a bun, push at each other till one of them has won!
1

Quicker than the wind and faster than a shark, she surfs on the waves until it gets dark.
5

Tiebreak, forehand, backhand, score. She swings her racket and scores some more!
2

When the ball flies high he gives it some clout, then runs super-fast so he won't get caught out.
6

ALIEN INVASION
WELL, WELL, WELL!
HERE COMES ANOTHER GUEST.
DING-DONG!

WELCOME TO OUR COSTUME PARTY, SAMURAI.

YOUR COSTUME IS FANTASTIC!
I HARDLY RECOGNIZED YOU.

DING-DONG!

AH! WHAT A MARVELLOUS ELF!
COME IN, PLEASE!

SOON WE'LL ANNOUNCE WHO WON
THE PRIZE FOR THE BEST COSTUME.

DING-DONG!

BEWARE, EARTHLINGS! I'M TAKING OVER YOUR PLANET! RESISTANCE IS FUTILE!

HEH, HEH, HEH! BRILLIANT! COME ON IN!

A MOMENT LATER . . .

COMMANDER! PLEASE REPORT THE INVASION STATUS!

MISSION ABORTED.
THE EARTHLINGS ARE A GREAT SOURCE OF FUN!
I'LL BE BACK IN A FEW DAYS. OVER AND OUT!

The Top Score

During archery training, this elf shot at four targets. Add up his scores and write them next to each target. Which target shows his best score?

Who's The Chief?

Only one small picture matches the big image of this Native American chief. Which one?

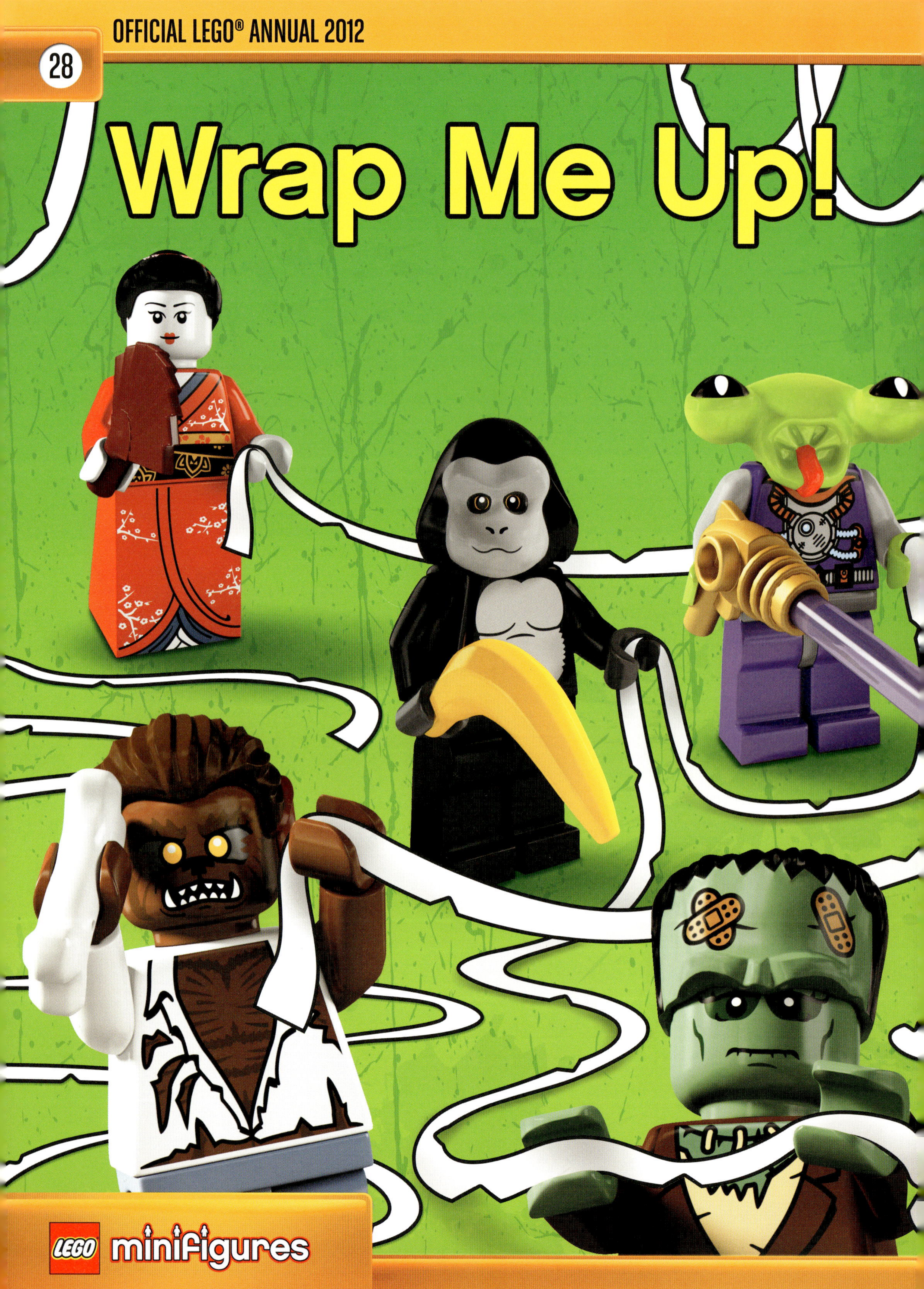
Wrap Me Up!
LEGO minifigures

Oops! This mummy accidentally unwrapped himself when he was playing with his pet scorpion! Luckily, he can always count on his friends. Can you work out who is helping to wrap him up again?
Now that's a wrap!

Out Of Time

There is something strange going on around the King's castle. Can you circle 10 things that don't belong in the picture?

Save The Princess

The brave knight must rescue the princess by climbing the tower – but he can only step on bricks that include the numbers 3 or 7. Can you draw a path for him to reach the top?

Catapult Fire!

The castle is under siege. Watch out for the missiles being shot from catapults! Can you draw a line that would divide the flying missiles into two equal sets?

Picture Puzzles

One of the King's knights is duelling with a Dragon Knight, while another is pursuing a prison carriage with a brave soldier captured by the enemy. Put the picture flags in the correct order to make the two amazing battle scenes.

MASTERS OF SPINJITZU

The four young ninja Masters of Spinjitzu are the saviours of Ninjago. Can you match these descriptions to each ninja? Write the correct numbers in the empty boxes.

This ninja is like fire – he's wild and dangerous. He's quick to act, quick to attack with his sword, and quick to get into big, big trouble. No wonder he is the Ninja of Fire.

This ninja is super-smart and super-fast. Swinging his favourite weapon, the nunchucks, he strikes the enemy like blue lightning. That's why he's called the Ninja of Lightning.

This is the leader of Sensei Wu's ninja team. He's a great warrior and a good friend. He always trains hard so as not to let down any of his friends during their mission. He's the Ninja of Earth.

This ninja is a seer with a sixth sense... and no sense of humour. He is cool, quiet and focused. He waits for the right time to crush the enemy like a white avalanche. He's the Ninja of Ice.

JAY
ZANE
KAI
COLE

THE RACE FOR THE WEAPON

Race against a friend! Each start at one end of the maze and draw a path as quickly as possible to the centre to decide who wins the Scythe of Quakes – the ninja or the skeleton warrior!

SKELETON
NINJA'S EXIT

ZANE'S BIRTHDAY
I HOPE ZANE WILL LIKE HIS BIRTHDAY CAKE!

I THINK I DESERVE A BREAK.

HEY!
THAT'S NOT FOR YOU!

LET'S GO, GUYS!
WE HAVE TO GET ZANE'S BIRTHDAY CAKE BACK!

WHAT'S GOING ON?
A PARTY WITHOUT ME?

WOW!
THAT WAS FUN! BUT WHERE'S
THE CAKE?
OVER THERE! IT'S GETTING AWAY!

HEH, HEH!
SAMUKAI WILL REWARD ME FOR
THIS CAKE!

HEY!

SLAP!

NO!

GUYS! WHY ARE YOU . . . ?

SPLAT!

ERM . . . HAPPY . . .
. . . BIRTHDAY TO YOU!
MMM! YUMMY!

ATTACK OF THE SKELETONS

General Nuckal and his skeletons are trying to steal another Golden Weapon of Spinjitzu. Can Sensei Wu and his ninjas protect the weapon and defeat the enemy? Take a good look at this scene – then turn the page to answer some questions!

道場
不屈
正義
忍者
忍者

TRUE OR FALSE?

How much can you remember from the picture on pages 42-43? Without looking back, answer the questions below by marking them "T" for "TRUE" or "F" for "FALSE".

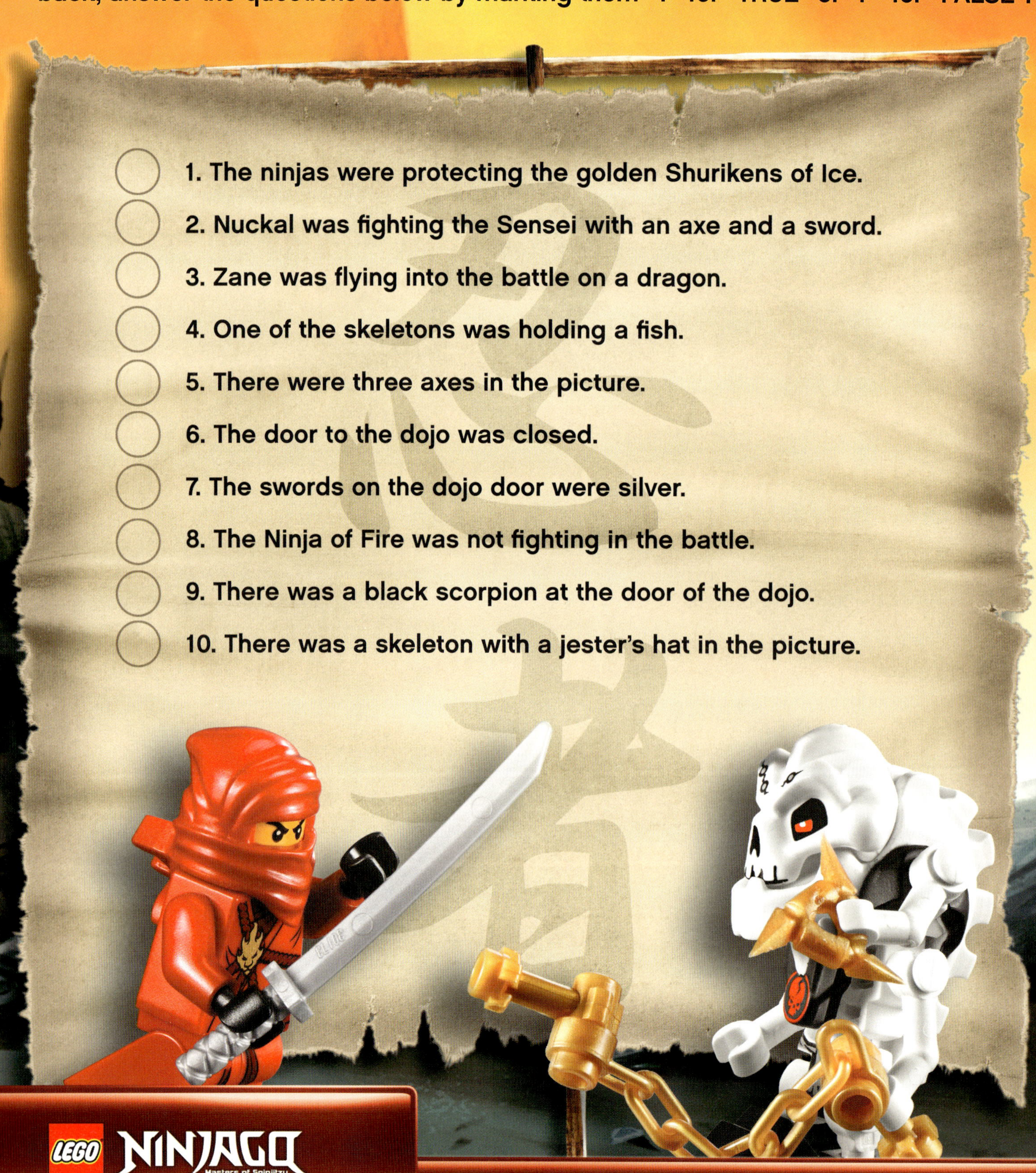

1. The ninjas were protecting the golden Shurikens of Ice.
2. Nuckal was fighting the Sensei with an axe and a sword.
3. Zane was flying into the battle on a dragon.
4. One of the skeletons was holding a fish.
5. There were three axes in the picture.
6. The door to the dojo was closed.
7. The swords on the dojo door were silver.
8. The Ninja of Fire was not fighting in the battle.
9. There was a black scorpion at the door of the dojo.
10. There was a skeleton with a jester's hat in the picture.

ODD ONE OUT

A true ninja has an eye for detail. Look at the pictures below and tick the odd one out in each row.

GARMADON'S FORTRESS

The brave ninja must get back the Weapons of Spinjitzu from Lord Garmadon's fortress. Find the pieces missing from the picture below and write the correct letters in the answer box.

1
2
3
4
5
3
4
5

WORDSEARCH

Find the last names of the hero robots in the wordsearch. How many times can you find "HERO FACTORY" in the grid? Watch out! The words may be written across, down, diagonally or backwards.

HERO FACTORY

NATHAN EVO
WILLIAM FURNO
JULIUS NEX
PRESTON STORMER
NATALIE BREEZ
MARK SURGE

Q	A	Z	W	S	X	E	E	D	C	R	F	V	T	G	B	H	Y
H	A	N	U	J	M	V	I	K	O	L	P	O	K	M	I	E	J
G	Y	B	H	E	R	O	F	A	C	T	O	R	Y	H	U	R	N
V	C	F	T	R	D	X	Z	S	E	W	A	Q	L	O	I	O	K
Q	A	Z	W	N	L	O	I	O	K	O	F	A	C	T	O	F	B
R	D	X	Z	E	R	D	X	Z	R	D	X	Z	N	H	E	A	N
E	H	F	H	X	A	N	E	O	S	U	R	G	E	F	B	C	A
N	E	R	D	X	Z	S	E	W	A	Q	L	R	B	S	R	T	K
V	R	E	M	R	O	T	S	X	Z	S	O	N	U	J	M	O	M
C	O	X	D	F	H	X	A	N	E	F	Q	A	Z	W	S	R	E
J	F	M	K	R	D	X	Z	N	A	U	F	H	X	A	N	Y	O
T	A	R	A	Q	A	Z	W	C	J	R	F	H	X	A	N	E	F
L	C	D	S	F	H	X	T	D	X	N	D	X	Z	Z	Q	G	Z
B	T	L	O	D	X	O	D	X	Z	O	B	R	E	D	X	Z	I
A	O	R	Z	G	R	F	H	X	A	N	E	E	F	H	X	A	X
Y	R	A	O	Y	F	H	X	A	N	E	R	Q	A	Z	W	S	E
Q	Y	Z	W	F	G	U	E	A	V	B	M	E	Q	U	P	S	C

THE NEW HEROES

Evo and Nex are the first two of the new type of heroes. Spot 10 differences between their final versions shown on the left hand page and the prototypes shown below.

MISSING ENDS

Work out the patterns in the sets of images on the next page. Which images from the top will complete each set? Write the correct letters in the empty spaces. Be careful! One image doesn't fit anywhere.

A
B
C
D
E
F
1
2
3
4
5

FIRE ALERT!

Fire Lord and his blistering-hot henchmen are a new threat to Hero Factory. Match the pieces of the villains' armour on the right to the characters below. Look carefully, though – one piece doesn't belong to any of them.

☐ JETBUG

☐ NITROBLAST

1
2
3
4
5
FIRE LORD
DRILLDOZER

Page 4
Countdown!

Page 6
Space Trail

Page 8
Wanted!

Page 15
At The Harbour

B

D

Page 20
Weird Science

The correct test tubes are C and D.

Page 21
Hidden Shapes

Page 22
Sports Rap!

1 – C, 2 – E, 3 – D,
4 – A, 5 – F, 6 – B.

Page 26
The Top Score

Page 27
Who's The Chief?

Picture D matches the big image.

Page 28
Wrap Me Up!

Page 30
Out Of Time

Page 32
Save The Princess

Page 33
Catapult Fire!

Page 34
Picture Puzzles

1 2 3 4

1 2 3 4

Page 36
MASTERS OF SPINJITZU

1 – Kai
2 – Jay
3 – Cole
4 – Zane

Page 38
THE RACE FOR THE WEAPON

Page 44
TRUE OR FALSE?

1 – T
2 – T
3 – F
4 – T
5 – F
6 – F
7 – F
8 – F
9 – T
10 – T

Page 45

ODD ONE OUT

Page 46

GARMADON'S FORTRESS

1 – A, 2 – G, 3 – I, 4 – B, 5 – D

Page 48

WORDSEARCH

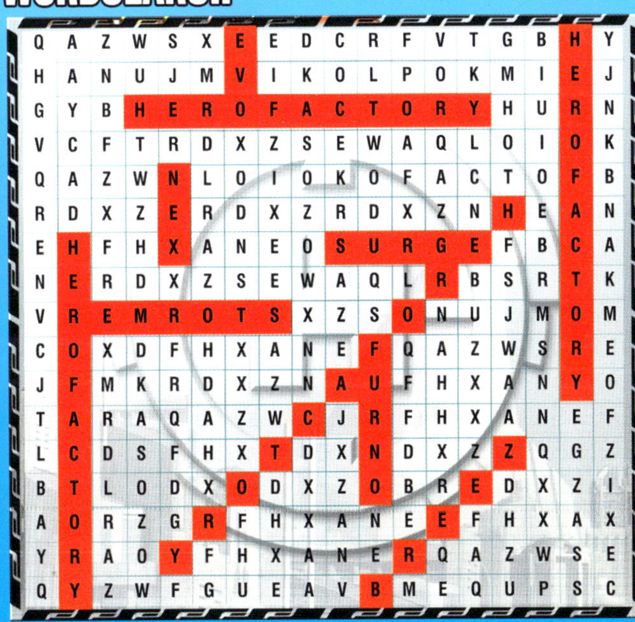

"Hero Factory" appears 4 times in this wordsearch.

Page 50

THE NEW HEROES

Page 52

MISSING ENDS

1 – E
2 – F
3 – B
4 – C
5 – A

Page 54

FIRE ALERT!

Nitroblast – 4
Jetbug – 2
Drilldozer – 1
Fire Lord – 3